P9-CML-298

The March From Selma to Montgomery

African Americans Demand the Vote

Jake Miller

The Rosen Publishing Group's
PowerKids Press™
New York

Published in 2004 by The Rosen Publishing Group, Inc.
29 East 21st Street, New York, NY 10010

First Edition

Editor: Frances E. Ruffin
Book Design: Emily Muschinske

Photo Credits: Cover and title page © Hulton/Archive/Getty Images; pp. 5, 6, 11, 20, 22 © Bettmann/CORBIS; p. 8 © Flip Schulke/CORBIS; pp. 8 (inset), 12, 16 © AP/Wide World; p. 15 © CORBIS; p. 19 © Library of Congress, Prints and Photographs Division.

Miller, Jake, 1969–
The march from Selma to Montgomery : African Americans demand the vote / Jake Miller.— 1st ed.
    p. cm. — (The library of the civil rights movement)
Includes bibliographical references and index.
Summary: Depicts the repeated efforts of civil rights advocates to march from Selma, Alabama, to Montgomery, only to be interrupted by national guardsmen.
  ISBN 0-8239-6254-7 (lib. bdg.)
1. Selma–Montgomery Rights March, 1965—Juvenile literature. 2. Selma (Ala.)—Race relations—Juvenile literature. 3. African Americans—Civil rights—Alabama—Selma—History—20th century—Juvenile literature. 4. African Americans—Suffrage—Alabama—Selma—History—20th century—Juvenile literature. 5. Civil rights movements—Alabama—Selma—History—20th century—Juvenile literature. [1. Selma–Montgomery Rights March, 1965. 2. African Americans—Civil rights. 3. Civil rights movements.] I.Title.
  F334.S4 M53 2003
    324.6'2'08996073—dc21
                                                2001007244

Manufactured in the United States of America

Contents

The Right to Vote

In a **democracy**, the people have the power. From our country's earliest days, white people have voted for the officials who run the government, from small-town mayors to the president of the United States. The Fifteenth **Amendment** to the U.S. **Constitution**, passed in 1870, gave black people the right to vote. However, in 1963, in Selma, Alabama, fewer than 400 of the 15,000 black people who were old enough to vote were registered. The white people who ran Selma's local government made it hard for blacks to register. Blacks had to take a test in order to sign up. The people who gave the test often cheated to make sure that blacks didn't pass. Several **civil rights** groups started voter registration drives in Alabama and in Mississippi. Dr. Martin Luther King Jr., a great civil rights leader, came to Selma in 1964.

Dr. Martin Luther King Jr. points to a map to show where black voters should be registered to vote.

Then and Now

In 1964, there were about 300 black elected officials in the entire United States. By January 1999, black and white people were able to vote for and elect 725 black officials in the state of Alabama alone.

Police Attack Protesters

Most of Selma's white politicians who controlled the city were afraid they would lose their power if blacks could vote. They tried to stop blacks from registering. When black people tried to register, the police often attacked or arrested them. To encourage blacks to register, Dr. Martin Luther King Jr. spoke at Brown Chapel, a church in Selma. To **protest** unfair arrests, groups of black people, and a few white supporters, marched in the streets of Selma and other nearby towns. At one point, more than 100 black teachers marched. On February 18, 1965, Alabama state troopers attacked a group of peaceful **demonstrators**. They beat the protesters with clubs. Jimmie Lee Jackson, a 26-year-old black man, was shot by the police. He was trying to stop them from beating his mother. Jackson died a few days later.

Left: Dr. King spoke at Brown Chapel in Selma, Alabama, to encourage black people to register to vote. Inset: More than 700 people attended Jimmie Lee Jackson's funeral.

A Bloody Sunday

To honor the memory of Jimmie Lee Jackson, **activists** planned to march from Selma to the state capital, Montgomery. They were going to demand that Governor George Wallace enable all of Alabama's citizens to vote. About 600 men, women, and children left Brown Chapel on Sunday March 7, 1965. As the peaceful marchers crossed the Edmund Pettus Bridge, the sheriff and 100 Alabama state troopers were waiting with gas masks and hard hats. The police told the marchers that they had 2 minutes to turn around. After just 1 minute, the police attacked the marchers with clubs and whips and trampled them with horses. Sixty-five marchers were hurt. That evening some television reporters referred to the events of that day as Bloody Sunday.

These photograph show marchers as they crossed the Edmund Pettus Bridge in Selma, Alabama. Inset: Moments later the sheriff and state troopers beat the marchers with clubs and bullwhips and shot tear gas at them.

Nationwide Support

That night a film of the attack played on national television news programs. On one channel, it interrupted a movie called *Judgment at Nuremberg*, which was a **documentary** about the trial of **Nazis** for war crimes they committed during **World War II** (1939–1945). Americans and their supporters fought the Nazis to protect freedom around the world. Viewers were shocked to see that some American citizens didn't have that freedom at home. Many northern white activists already supported the civil rights cause. Some came to the South to work on voting rights campaigns. They saw for themselves why many blacks were afraid of their own cities' police. When news films about Bloody Sunday in Selma played on television, the whole nation saw how unfair the struggle was for black people.

Alabama state troopers wrestle student civil rights leader John Lewis to the ground and beat him during a protest march at Montgomery, the state capital of Alabama.

Turn-Around Tuesday

Dr. Martin Luther King Jr. had been preaching at his church in Atlanta, Georgia, when he heard about the attack. He started making plans to attempt another march for the following Tuesday. About 1,400 people, black and white, came to Selma from around the country to join the march. King and the other organizers tried to get a judge's permission to march. The judge told them that he needed time to think about their request. King led the march as far as the bridge where, again, state troopers were lined up. King said a prayer and then turned the march around. He stopped the march to avoid more **violence**, but that night a group of local white people attacked a white Boston minister named James Reeb. He had come to Selma for the march. He died soon after.

Demonstrators, led by Dr. Martin Luther King Jr., marched to the Edmund Pettus Bridge, where they saw troopers lined up.

Changing Times

On Monday March 15, 1965, President Lyndon B. Johnson spoke to the U.S. Congress. He said that the violence that was happening in Selma was un-American and terribly wrong. He said that black people struggling for voting rights was neither a black problem nor a southern problem. It was a problem for all Americans. He said that the civil rights protesters were freedom fighters. He announced plans for a new law that would enable blacks in the South to vote. His law would get rid of unfair tests. Two days later, a federal judge gave the people in Selma permission to march to Montgomery. He forbade the state police from interfering, and he promised to protect the marchers from more violence. President Johnson addressed the U.S. Congress about the Voting Rights Act of 1965, on March, 15, 1965.

Martin Luther King Jr. met with President Johnson. At the end of his speech to Congress on March 15, 1965, President Johnson said, "We shall overcome!" These were the words used by civil rights demonstrators.

Then and Now

The Civil Rights movement was not the only movement that had people marching in the streets during the 1960s. Thousands of Americans marched for the rights of women and farm workers, and against war.

Crossing the Bridge

On Sunday March 21, 1965, Dr. Martin Luther King Jr. began the march from Brown Chapel in Selma. Along with John Lewis, leader of the Student Nonviolent Coordinating Committee (SNCC), King led more than 3,000 marchers along the river to the bridge. The marchers were black and white, students and preachers, housewives and activists. They were also writers, artists, and movie stars. They walked arm in arm. Once again the marchers were surrounded by men in uniform, but this time the officers were there to protect the marchers. There were soldiers from the Alabama national guard and the U.S. Army. There were also U.S. Marshals and **agents** from the Federal Bureau of Investigation (FBI). They checked bridges and fields along the way for bombs and made sure that no one would attack the marchers.

Marchers crossed the Edmund Pettus Bridge on the first day of a five-day walk to Montgomery, Alabama. They were joined by people of all races from many different cities and states around the country.

The Long March

The march was about 58 miles (93 km) long. It passed through farmlands and small towns. It was not always easy going. The marchers covered about 12 miles (19 km) each day. They walked through rainstorms. At night the temperature fell below freezing. The marchers slept in tents pitched in schoolyards, muddy cow pastures, and other places. Many walked with blisters on their feet, but they continued. They were proud of what they were doing. As they marched, they sang **spirituals** and **freedom songs**. On the fourth day of the march, they were treated to a concert by famous popular entertainers. Folk singers Joan Baez, Peter, Paul and Mary, and Harry Belafonte, and recording stars Johnny Mathis and Sammy Davis Jr. were among those who marched and sang.

Black teenagers joined the march to Montgomery. Inset: These muddy shoes show that during their five-day walk to Montgomery, the marchers walked during sunny and rainy weather, on dry and muddy roadways.

Arriving in Montgomery

After five days of walking, the marchers reached Montgomery on March 25, 1965. They walked straight to the Alabama state capitol building for a huge **rally**. By then there were some 25,000 marchers. Dr. Martin Luther King Jr. and other leaders gave speeches. Many other important leaders of the Civil Rights movement were there, including Rosa Parks. She was one of the heroes of the Montgomery Bus Boycott, which began with her arrest in 1955. The movement for civil rights had come a long way in those 10 years, but the struggle was far from finished. Later that day, a white volunteer named Viola Liuzzo was driving a group of marchers back to Selma after the rally when she was shot and killed by a group of **racists**.

When the marchers arrived at the Alabama state capitol building, they broke out American flags to show that black people, too, were Americans, and that they should have the right to vote.

Walking Toward Freedom

On August 3, 1965, Congress passed the Voting Rights Act of 1965. On August 6, President Johnson signed the act into law. The new law removed the unfair tests that prevented blacks from registering to vote. President Johnson also sent special government workers to states with low numbers of registered black voters to help people sign up quickly. By September 1965, more than 50,000 new voters were added in Alabama, Mississippi, and Louisiana. Before 1965, southern blacks were locked out of our democracy, because they could not vote. Today they have the ability to participate in choosing our government. Every step down the road from Selma to Montgomery was a long march toward freedom.

In 1965, many African Americans in the South were able to register to vote for the first time. The people in this photograph gathered to register in Peachtree, Alabama.

Glossary

activists (AK-tih-vists) People who take action for what they believe is right.

agents (AY-jents) People who are given the power to represent another person or the government.

amendment (uh-MEND-mint) An addition or change to the Constitution.

civil rights (SIH-vul RYTS) The rights of citizens guaranteed by law.

Constitution (kahn-stih-TOO-shun) The basic rules by which the United States is governed.

democracy (dih-MAH-kruh-see) A government that is run by the people who live under it.

demonstrators (DEH-mun-stray-terz) People who take part in a march or a meeting to protest or to make demands to bring about change.

documentary (dah-kyoo–MEN-tuh-ree) A movie or a television program about real people and events.

freedom songs (FREE-dum SONGZ) Songs that were sung during civil rights marches.

Nazis (NOT-zees) During World War II, members of the German army under the leadership of Adolf Hitler.

protest (PRO-test) An act of disagreement to bring about change.

racists (RAY-sists) Those who believe that one race or nationality is inferior to another.

rally (RA-lee) A large gathering of people who come together for a common purpose.

spirituals (SPEER-ih-chuh-wulz) Religion-based songs in the United States, mainly sung by southern African Americans.

violence (VY-lents) Rough or harmful action.

World War II (WURLD WOR TOO) A war fought between the United States, Great Britain, and Russia, and Germany, Japan, and Italy from 1939 to 1945.

Index

Primary Sources

Cover: Dr. Martin Luther King Jr. speaking to followers on March 9, 1965. **Page 5**: Dr. King making plans for the march to Montgomery, Alabama (January 1965). **Page 6**: Dr. King speaking at Brown Chapel in Selma, Alabama (February 1965). **Page 6 (inset)**: The funeral procession for Jimmie Lee Jackson in Marion, Alabama (March 1965). **Page 8**: Civil rights marchers crossing the Edmund Pettus Bridge in Selma. By Flip Schulke (1965). **Page 11**: SNCC leader John Lewis is wrestled to the ground and injured in front of the state capitol in Montgomery, Alabama. From United Press International. **Page 12**: Alabama state troopers beat and use tear gas against marchers on Bloody Sunday March 7, 1965. From Associated Press. **Page 12 (inset)**: Marchers are turned back on the Pettus Bridge (March 1965). From Associated Press. **Page 15**: Dr. Martin Luther King Jr. and President Lyndon B. Johnson meet. (1964). **Page 16**: Marchers stream across the Pettus Bridge on March 12, 1965. From Associated Press. **Page 19**: Black teenagers sing as they march to Montgomery. From UPI (1965). **Page 19 (inset)**: A marcher's muddy shoes. From UPI (1965). **Page 20**: Marchers arrive at Montgomery state capitol. (1965).

Web Sites

Due to the changing nature of Internet links, PowerKids Press has developed an online list of Web sites related to the subject of this book. This site is updated regularly. Please use this link to access the list:

www.powerkidslinks.com/lcrm/marselm/